A WINNING SKILLS BOOK

You Can Handle Rude People!

Joy Berry

Illustrated by Bartholomew

Joy Berry Enterprises

Copyright © Joy Berry, 2022
Originally Published 2013

All rights are reserved.

No part of this book can be duplicated or used without the prior written permission of the copyright owner, except for the use of brief quotations from the book.

For inquiries or permission requests contact the publisher.

Published by Joy Berry Enterprises
www.joyberryenterprises.com

Joy Berry
Enterprises

You can get along with rude people by
- understanding why getting along with some people can be difficult,
- understanding why some people are rude,
- knowing why you need to learn how to deal with rude people,
- following eight steps to getting along, and
- remembering three wise sayings.

A majority of people are kind and helpful. Therefore, getting along with most people is easy.

However, some people are not kind and helpful. Getting along with these people can be difficult.

WHY GETTING ALONG CAN BE DIFFICULT

There are several reasons why getting along with some people can be difficult.

Some people are difficult to get along with because they are **self-centered.**

People who are self-centered do not care about others as much as they care about themselves. They can be greedy, selfish, and unfair. Self-centered people usually take more from other people than they give to them.

Some people are difficult to get along with because they have a **superior attitude.**

People with superior attitudes think that they are better than other people. They act as though they know more and can do more than others. People with superior attitudes often try to make the people around them feel inferior.

Some people are difficult to get along with because they are **bossy.**

People who are bossy try to control others. They tell people around them what to do and expect them to do as they're told. Bossy people are bad sports when things do not happen the way that they want them to happen.

Some people are difficult to get along with because they **bully** others.

People who are bullies like to frighten or hurt others who are smaller or weaker than they are. They try to solve their problems by threatening or fighting with others.

Some people are difficult to get along with because they are **offensive.**

People who are offensive do not care about the thoughts and feelings of other people. They do things that hurt or insult others. Offensive people often cause those around them to be uncomfortable.

Some people are difficult to get along with because they are **negative.**

People who are negative are never satisfied. They whine and complain about everyone and everything. Negative people say things and do things that make themselves and the people around them unhappy.

Some people are difficult to get along with because they are **irresponsible.**

People who are irresponsible do not do what they are supposed to do. They often fail to keep their commitments. Irresponsible people disappoint the people who depend on them.

Some people are difficult to get along with because they are **stubborn.**

People who are stubborn have a hard time compromising or giving in to others. They have difficulty admitting that they are wrong or saying that they are sorry. Stubborn people often cause other people to feel frustrated.

Some people are difficult to get along with because they are **unresponsive.**

People who are unresponsive act as though they are not interested in others. They do not do their part to keep a conversation going. They have a hard time sharing feelings with others. Communicating with unresponsive people is not easy.

Some people are difficult to get along with because they are **insincere.**

People who are insincere are phony. They pretend to be someone other than who they are. Their actions and words do not show how they truly think and feel. It is hard to trust insincere people.

WHY SOME PEOPLE ARE RUDE

Some people feel and act the way they do for several reasons.

Some people are rude because they are ignorant.

They have not learned acceptable behavior. They do not know the correct way to act.

Some people are rude because they have personal problems.

They have problems in their lives that are not being solved. They act the way that they do because their problems cause them to be frustrated and upset.

Some people are rude because they feel inferior.

They do not feel that they are as good as other people. They act the way that they do to try to prove that they are as good, or better than others.

Some people are rude because they need attention.

They need to have people notice them. They act the way that they do so that others will pay attention to them.

Some people are rude because they are afraid.

They are afraid that other people might hurt them in some way. They act the way that they do so that people will fear them and not bother them.

Some people are rude because they are angry.

They are angry about something that has upset them. They express their anger by being unkind.

Learning how to get along with rude people is necessary because you are likely to come in contact with rude people often.

Some of the rude people that you encounter are people you know. You might be around these people often.

No matter how often you are around a rude person, he or she can upset you.

Rude people can make your life unpleasant if you don't know how to deal with them.

If you do not want rude people to make your life unpleasant, you need to respond the them in a positive way. Here are eight steps to help you do this:

Step 1: Try to understand rude people

Try to understand **why** rude people act the way that they do. Try to find out whether they
- are ignorant,
- have personal problems,
- feel inferior,
- need attention,
- are afraid, or
- are angry.

Do these things to learn about a rude person whom you encounter frequently:
- Put yourself in the other person's place. Try to imagine how you would think and act if you were that person.
- Talk directly to the person.
- Talk to people who know the person well.

Step 2: Accept rude people the way they are.

Do not try to change other people. Realize that changing someone else is impossible. People can only change themselves.

You can accept someone who is rude more easily if you remember that every person has good qualities. Discover and concentrate on the good qualities about a person rather than on his or her faults.

Step 3: Forgive rude people.

Hate and anger are powerful emotions. They can cause you to be upset and can make you very unhappy. When you hate other people or stay angry at them, you are hurting yourself.

When you forgive someone, the hate or anger you feel for the person often goes away. You usually feel better and so does the person you forgive. Understanding someone who is rude and accepting that person makes it easier for you to forgive him or her.

Step 4: Be kind to rude people.

Do whatever you can to assure people that you do not want to hurt them in any way. If you are kind and supportive, people will most likely feel comfortable around you and will not need to act in a negative way.

Do whatever you can to make people feel good about themselves. Compliment them. Encourage them so that they will not need to get attention in negative ways.

Step 5: Talk to rude people about their behavior.

Tell them in a kind way just how you feel about their misbehavior. Tell them about how it affects you. Ask them to stop doing what they are doing.

When you talk to a rude person about his or her misbehavior, try to do these things:
- Talk to the person when you are calm so that you do not say things that you might regret.
- Talk to the person when he or she is not upset.
- Talk to the person when he or she has time to listen to you.
- Talk to the person face to face, and look into his or her eyes when you talk.

Step 6: Do not take rude people's behavior personally.

Do not assume something is wrong with you when someone treats you badly. Remember, a rude person's misbehavior is his or her problem, not yours.

Following these six steps will probably help you feel better. Also, if you respond in a positive way to someone who is rude, he or she may stop misbehaving. However, if a rude person does not change, you need to follow two additional steps.

Step 7: Do not pay attention to rude people when they are misbehaving.

Try to ignore rude people when they treat you badly. Do not react to their misbehavior.

It is harder for someone to upset you or to make your life unpleasant if you ignore the person.

Step 8: Avoid being around rude people.

As much as possible, stay away from people who treat you badly. This makes it harder for them to bother you.

It might be hard to avoid being around a rude person whom you must see often, such as teacher, coach, or relative. To avoid such a person, you might need to ask an adult whom trust to help you.

Tell the adult exactly how you feel about the rude person. Ask for help in deciding whether or not you should avoid the rude person. If you agree that the person should be avoided, ask the adult for advice on how you can avoid being around the person.

Here are three wise sayings that can help you learn to get along with rude people:

Saying #1: A soft word turns away wrath.

Speaking kindly to an angry person might help him or her to calm down. You might be able to help the person overcome the anger that is making him or her a rude person. In this way, you are doing a favor for everyone.

Saying #2: You can't fight fire with fire.

You cannot put out a fire with fire. A fire must be put out with something else, such as water. It is the same with negative behavior. You cannot stop a person from being unkind by being unkind yourself. You cannot stop an argument by arguing.

To stop negative behavior, you must respond in a positive way.

Saying #3: Be kind to your enemies, and you won't have any.

It is hard to be unkind to someone who is being kind to you. It is hard to hate someone who is caring toward you. When you are kind and caring to someone, you make it hard for that person to hate and mistreat you. Instead, the person is encouraged to like you and to treat you well.

Sometimes you might find it difficult to be kind to a person who is cruel to you. However, it is not impossible. In most cases, kindness usually is the only thing that works with a rude person. Being cruel to someone who is being cruel only makes the person want to become more cruel. Kindness is powerful and has the potential to overcome cruelty.

CONCLUSION

Rude people are a part of everyone's life. You can get along with these people if you learn how to respond to them in a positive way.

www.ingramcontent.com/pod-product-compliance
Lightning Source LLC
Chambersburg PA
CBHW081409070526
44583CB00020B/2733